Epiphanies

Poems of Liberation, Exile and Confinement

Harvey Gillman

ISBN: 978-1-8383850-0-2

Layout and design: Compositions by Carn.
www.compsbycarn.co.uk

Cover photo: Trish Carn

Contents

Introduction

Questions

They asked him: 'What do you believe?'

He replied: 'We are alive together on this fragile earth. What we do has meaning and consequences. We can fail and fall. We can love and nurture.'

They asked him: 'What is the light you talk about?'

He replied: 'It shines sometimes. It casts a shadow. It reveals. It warms. It burns. It may be found in the heart of each but is owned by none.'

They asked him: 'What is your faith?'

He replied: 'The light will shine even when our eyes are closed through sleep or blinded by fear.'

They asked him: 'What is your prayer?'

He replied: 'To keep my arms open. And my heart. And my eyes. That my lips may sometimes move.'

They asked him: 'What would you die for?'

He replied: "My question is rather, 'For what, for whom do I live this day, this hour?'"

They asked him: 'What is your God?'

He replied: 'The creative silence that welcomes beyond the edge of words. The light that burns in the darkness. The wind that is my breath, our breath, blowing where it wills. God is not the name of God and the wind has no name and blows through the doors and the windows of many temples.'

They asked him: 'What is your authority?'

He replied: 'The restless communion of the winding path. Visited sometimes by grace.'

They asked him: 'What happens when we are dead?'

He replied: 'Death has taught me a concern for life, for open doors, and arching bridges. For the challenge of this moment, for the challenge of this transient life. Moments of unknowing. Glimmers of more. A discovery.'

They asked him: 'What have you learned in your seventy years?'

He replied; 'We are not just our names, our past, our spoken and written words. We are all anointed. Our country, our deepest faith, has no flag, no borders. We may be each other's purgatory or hell, or even paradise.'

They asked him: 'What is your hope?'

He replied: 'That we may continue to cherish our questions, cherish each other. That we be not afraid to be silent with each other. That in spite of the pain we and the day inflict upon each other, we still can believe, have faith, pray, and even dare to love. My hope is that we go on hoping, though our hearts and our history and the shadows of the moon may teach us to give up hope. That despair may not be the last word.'

First steps

Ill in Cherbourg

Blue clouds leap across the sky
over blue walls and stalls of flowers.
The sun melts brilliantly into pools of rain.
Through the windows, the clatter of midday plates.
The descending of stairs,
the silence of a stranger,
a heaven empty of angels.

View from Marseilles

There was a child
who read in large books
of certain principalities
where pines grew tall
over blue ruins.

An older man
watched the nightboats
returning
to spread their meagre catch
in the moonlight.

The Minstrel and the Estaque

The sea as green as your voice
surges into my dreams tonight.
It is clear like the songs you sang
echoing music of long ago.
My siren, you search the mists of my brain.
In your eyes I saw the moon over the port,
the crags and the broken beaches.
In your voice I heard melodies
we could have sung together
as the sun sank orange in the tired west,
songs of naive revolution for that new day
when such minstrelsy would be superfluous.

To a passer-by

We are not saints.
Do not condemn us to martyrdom.

In our rhetoric we have said
sanctity is easy
obeys its own rules
needs no invention.

But there is that other sanctity
born at the moment when
hand shuts door
foot descends stair
train leaves finally
sun lines roof with crimson.

That is more difficult

Myths and legends

Dare I
this I
quite give up
walk away
from the raft
to walk on land,
on sand that
may be the sun
shining on the sea
land that
may be land
but quick and swallowing?

Dare I
move on,
shipwrecked here,
discover my island
and its inhabitant?

Is this land
another myth
to add to the many
archipelagos of encounter
between man and islands.
islands and islands,
man and man?

It was your voice...

It was your voice made a nest in memory when
in a moment of despair, discretion gone,
in that dark place, seizing the loneliness
at the bottom of the glass, words broke forth,
heavy with drink, words like rings to yoke
in eternal covenant your silence to mine
and we swapping memories like photographs
of faces and ports we passed without knowing.

Then my ghostbird you flew, the dawn breaking,
the dark cage of night leaving my ark adrift
in troubled waters for the day to calm them.
You flew on paradise wings, sailed the grey ocean
leaving a voice, the echo of a touch,
the perhaps of a return, never consummated.

To my parents

When he saw her lying there
at the foot of the table,
a gash on her old skin, he knelt down
and touched the white strands of hair
he rarely caressed by day before.
He kissed her hands and called
a name that was known to him alone.

(That day I wore an orchid –
my only day of flowers.
I felt my bones so fragile,
your skin so soft, the slightest stone
could have shattered us).

He lay beside her on the floor
and rocked her in his arms.
(They were together then
under a canopy of flowers
and snow was falling
as he gave her the ring.)
With this ring I exchange
your death for mine.

Der Rebbe

The old man opened wide his eyes when the shy young man told him his name.

Rain was falling on the cold house.

'Once,' the old man said, 'I had much affection for you, though you lost yours for me.

The younger man sat down on the hard bench as years before.

The old man spoke of old stories: when the messiah would come, and why we must remain in exile.

The younger man watched him, noted the tone of voice.

He was a child again, swaying in prayer over tattered books packed with commentary.

'So what do you remember after all this time?' the rebbe asked.

'It always rained', I replied, as the drops beat against the walls between us.

Poems of Preparation

Winter jasmine

Thin, taut within the frame
that tied it to the world
it grew, and grew tall.
Planted once to fill a patch
between one rose and another –
it was perhaps an afterthought.

Pruned after the last increase of flower,
it lay still and hidden under the dry leaves
that fell one night. Its roots grew deep,
its stem grew thick. It filled inside with longing.

Then one morning, unseen, uncalled for,
it quickened, opened out yellower
than the sun against the black sharp earth.

Crucified against the cold wall,
it burst to flower.
It witnessed in its vigil
against the hardness and the harshness
of a winter of a world

and waited
in the cycle of its love.

Lines written at Quarr

There are lives.
Shall I give me to them?
The sea glows by my transparent skin.
There is a flame
where my blood is.

Still the bells
beat out the old self
beat in the new.
The air ripples my hair
like a lover.

The sun on warm glass,
blue, red on cold stone.
Pour me like water
over the blue clay.
Temper me

in the heat of your love.
In me shall grow then
Edens. The sword of angels
holds in the spirit
of the god hovering.

Plant the pips
of new apples
in the depths of my eyes.
Open me with marvels
and I shall praise.

Resurrection, a love poem.

Wait for me, he begged.
Wait for me there by the door,
half-open to the glass-sharp light.

Do not speak.
Do not even lift your hand to me,
though you see pain thorn-deep
across the mound of my skull.

Close your eyes for me
and when I rise
hold me firmly in your heart
and in the sinews of your arms.

Do not let me fall
broken to earth.

Lift me loving
from the tomb they would consign me.
Do not fasten me to stone
– oh bear me with you.

And then
patiently
suddenly
swiftly
I shall kiss you to new life.

Plena gratia

She smiles serenely.
Candles flicker.
Desires, hopes, terror
flicker, splutter.
Wax forms pools
like memory on black spikes.

Hail Miriam,
mother of bitter waters.
Hail Miriam,
sister of fears.
Hail Miriam,
daughter of multitudes.

Hail child
green in hope,
bruised mother of departures.
We shine, break, burn,
melt before you.

Hail mother,
sister of my brothers
and of my sisters.
You burn before us,
wood of our ecstasy.
Hail daughter
of our crucified children.

Hail tender,
holding out my brother,
a child laughing
at the tears of night,
child playing
with pain.

Hail Miriam,
lover, mother,
of each of my lovers.
I burn like a candle.
We flicker and melt
in transfiguration.

Hail Miriam,
Mother, sister, lover.
We are reborn
in our loving.
We are midwives
to the world.

Seed of fire

Filled with new life,
ready with seed,
they buried him.

The bark of him flogged,
roots cut loose
into fertile earth.

In a dark place,
the seed bursts,
hidden.

A well-meaning woman
had thought him the gardener,
not the gardened.

After many days
when forgetting grew,
they met in fear.

Away from the crowds,
they sacrificed disconsolately
on habitual altars.

Now in the damp
catacombs of our hearts
where once we stored
debris of expectations

an ashen
seed erupts
into new green.

Colours of the rainbow

The guards gave out the colours.
(I always loved rainbows).
They took out a large knife, cut the rainbow in pieces.
Triangles of brightness fell from the sky,
fell from the sky like snow on the mud
fell like stars of blood on our heads
in Auschwitz, in Dachau, in Sachsenhausen,
in Treblinka, in Ravensbruck, in Buchenwald.
Stars of yellow for the Jews
patches of red for the politicals
green for the criminals
black for anti-socials
purple for Jehovah's Witnesses
blue for emigrants
brown for gypsies
triangles of pink for homosexuals.

Flowers of brightest death.
Here, my love, is our bouquet of bitter herbs,
gather them, gather them.
We shall reclaim
from the stones and the ditches
from the ovens and the forests
a new patchwork of colour
and cover what remains of our lovers,
our friends, our accomplices,
our sisters, the small children of our dreams.

Next year perhaps, in the city of peace
we shall come to the altar
in garments of multicoloured flame
each with her song
each with his melody
and we shall sing
a new covenant
in fire of yellow red green black purple blue pink.
The letters shall burn deep
into the rock of every broken heart.

Frank's song

The dead have a pact with us.
Though tombs lie fallow in fields of snow
and our feet break on dried-out clay,
they wait with us. They bear messages
on days even of great sunlight
when shadow are as short as memories.

And so you return, smiling in a photograph,
a sheepish, unassuming inward sort of smile.
Did it hover as they drugged you
to smother your rage, your joy, your fear
of finding yourself alone in another sort of world,
the smile that was your wall, your welcome?

All things touch, the living and the dead.
We smile, we love, we pass.
We embrace with such a force
no warmth remains except
traces of breath in the air,
sweat on the hair,
the smell of fear.

With the prints of our fingertips
we have signed on the skin of the whole world
vast covenants of loving.
We bear each other the messages of our flesh
and of our silences.
Nothing can divide us now.

Poems of Pilgrimage and of Retreat

Walsingham

Miriam,
young girl of bitter waters, we have come
far, you and I, from our particular ghettoes
to meet in this place where wind and swans
rustle among the late summer foliage.
We have both gone down to Egypt with our broods
of expectations. On our return we have been counted
among the dour statistics of asylum seekers.

Here
they have built you a house and set you
in plaster, ever gazing, ever gracious,
at your first son's first stretching out
to his dark world. Miriam, there must have been times
when you wished him away with other children,
away from the broken pieces of his father's wood.
There must have been days under the fig-tree
when other angels brooded and other girls whispered
and other children built castles of dust
from the dry soil.

Mother,
they have taken you and stilled your yearning,
coated you in cool blue, you, who loved reds
and yellows and emerald tunics.
In your name they have taken your brothers and sisters,
have bled them in the cold marble morning

have taken your children, have nailed up their fingers,
have burned them, and scattered them.

And so we meet
in this unlikely place you have made a home,
daughter of laughter, daughter and sister,
in this lush oasis on our interrupted journey,
an oasis between miracles. On this altar then
I offer you this burning. I cannot wipe away
these tears, you cannot put out this fire.
Together fire and water we touch. We stand on earth
and hold the air, all elements seethe with praise and
lamentation.

Miriam,
I offer you these wild late-summer flowers
from all the hedgerows of all the lanes
we have passed through together. And for a moment
I stand before you to garland your black Jewish hair:
with this makeshift rosary of pain and love.

Prayer

My God, I stand before you now,
an average sensual man,
trembling still at the sight of beauty,
at the promise of passion,
having stood and sat and lain
in so many postures of adulation,
supplication and penitence.

I stand before you
bearing incense and memories,
grudges and inspirations.
I quiver still at the smell of blood,
my own and the blood I've shed,
to appease various intoxications.

Your light within my cage
casts long pools of darkness.
Yet still I stand before you,
fist clenched, fist reaching out,
a curse and then a blessing,
an angel and a scattering of dust.

and what if....

and what if every leaf were a thought of God,
every bud thrusting forth from the mind of God,
every blade of grass, every ring of wood, every note
of every bird, reflections on the wing of every fly,
moth, bee, wren, sparrow, pigeon, heron and hawk,
every growing thing and every passing thing,
every flash of dark in sunlight, every fading thing,
and falling thing and dying thing and stalk and leaf
were thoughts of God exploding with green sap and grace?

And what if every thought of God were skin and limb
and hair, and forms were flung from the mind of God,
and sprouted like lilies on the face of God?
How then would it be if we sat in the laughter of God
and opened our dry hearts to the waters like hart
at the cool brook, like thirsty cats by a garden pond?
How would it be for us, fleshed out forms of the passion of
God,
if we but turned and turned again with opened arms, our
breath
the inspiring of God, the generous embracing of God with
God?

Poems of blue

1

On this dark blue morning,
I have seen a moon so intense
illuminate a velvet sky.
I never felt so strong
the pull on the soul
like the drag of the sea.
In such a moon
a life could drown
with open throat
in an ecstasy of light.

2

A winter sky of such tenderness
aches on the dark body of the earth.
Oh, but we do not see,
the heart fades between catastrophes.
We engage somewhat with everyday horror.
The shell of the world is so blue,
it hurts to see, not to see.

3

I sat in adoration of the moon
pulled by light into an embrace
I had not known before, like a face of god
massive, unsmiling,
the planets of its heart on offer,

distant cool like a judging god,
radiant with white heat,
lighting up something almost lost
in a landscape of flesh and wood.

4
It was a sky to swim across
a ritual bath of a heaven
blue for redemption
for drowning.

The temptation

It's not what you are
(how should I know?)
but that upon you remains
some vestige of Eden,
half remembered,
dreamed about.

You – child before the fall,
handful of red earth,
from which my bones came also,
when the race was one,
before the snake of intrigue
bade us eat of knowledge.
It is the return that tempts me
back before the cross-sword of angels.
Your face to remind me
that it was good to walk
in the cool of the evening,
naked and unashamed.

She chose the stone

The Word
has disappeared into
Flesh; become implicate, folded
into the tapestry of things.

Ordinary it is
– you and me and they,
the warp and weft of
encounter.

Why then weigh
and measure
flesh into
another theology?

Let it find its own
words,
speak its own
silence.

Deer. A Vision

On the hill
beyond the wall
through the clearing
he does not come today.
Perhaps it is the soft rain
that makes him hide
– or that I long too much
for his gracious visit.
It would no longer be
an unexpected vision.

Yesterday he sauntered down
through the greygreen woods
to browse along the path,
a bud, a shoot, some grass
following some atavistic smell.
Then satisfied he slowly turned
with the gentle nobility
of a regal ghost, climbed back
to the sky beyond the hill,
leaving me with the gift
of his absence.

Seven poems on retreat

1

Where do the words go when they have been uttered,
when they have passed into heart and memory?
It is so easy to let them go, arrows shot skilfully
around targets of desire. They have been so many,
so easy, so quick – words from a deep place,
a fissure in the rock. Yet silence is a fearful place.
It throbs. It causes a trembling of limbs. It is so heavy.
It knows. It is the arrow and the bow,
the arm, the heart, the blood that is already flowing.

2

My hosts have provided me with keys for the inner and outer
doors.
I have locked my heart's chamber already, but what lies
therein
cannot be guarded against. I bring in my enemy, my
restlessness.
The bell chimes the monks to worship.
I shall not go tonight to the chapel where the wood has split,
nor receive the sprinkling blessing of herbs in water.
Prayers of protection will not protect me
from dreams that lie with me
on the counterpane like feral cats.

3

I have unlearnt to pray.
I lose the words. I lose the directions

of the heart. I do not attend. The silence
echoes my silence. I carry inside
scraps of many prayers. Each paper
is scribbled upon and torn. Some are heavy
with the crumbled stone of wailing walls.
Out of this emptiness may rise
perhaps some expression of blood
or water. There still is the blood.
There still is flesh. There still is bone.
Will you grace bone to an instrument?
Will you play? Will you not teach me
new tunes and dances? Will you not?

4
When the light went out,
I would have wanted a single candle
to light up my cell,
something romantic, monastic,
a touch medieval perhaps?
Something perhaps that did not light up
the wayward etchings upon my skin.
But the moon lights up a mirror.
There is no way out
from the world outside, the world within.
The light marks the soul with a sculptor's knife,
proves the heart does not end
with the winding contours of the skin.

5

In the courtyard the blue virgin holds her child close.
She faces the fountain, looks beyond the horizon.
They are both cold tonight. She looks over the child's head.
The sky is a different blue, rich, intense, possessed of an
immensity.
I watch her from my cell. The fountain falls silent.
She waits for adoration, for the child who sits,
so well behaved upon her lap. She knows the waiting
will not last. The evening air moves.
The leaves tremble. The fountain has fallen silent.
Her child sits slightly forward also waiting.

6

On this new morning the grass has begun to speak
prompted by a return of sunlight.
Slowly it unwinds syllables which lead to music.
There is a whispering through rain and winter.
I listen to the sky unfolding. The trees
climb out of their nakedness.

7

But the new words are not the words I have used before.
The old words have come and gone
to their small places, to their allotted time.
They were not the lessons of the grass and of the trees,
not the teachings of the rain nor the wind's examples.

Now in the chapel by the rough-hewn table,
we stand together. Our minds are emptied, our hearts half-
tamed.
Wine passes round in spirals of incense.
Rain beats on the roof where the new wood has already
cracked.
The bread of the heart crumbles, crumbles,
is picked upon by the birds of heaven.

This, among the swaying grass, the wind, the gales of dreams,
is the word we offer,
this the sign of peace that is more than sign.
This proffering by each to each of the burnished cup
is the peace, the love, the fear acknowledged
and, for a moment, the separation overcome.

El Morche, March 2005

All weekend I have listened to the sea,
have risen with the sea,
have slept with the sea,
have walked along the changing shoreline.

The sun has risen, has set.
The earth has changed its colours,
the sky its colours, the voice its colours.
The earth has groaned under the weight of the sea.

I do not speak the language of the sea.
Mine is an earth language, stuttering,
a language which with its nets
trawls the sky and stars and brings in the wind.

On the sand now lie broken clauses.
Verbs collect in pools.
Nouns lie scattered.
Earth and water sparkle with exclamation marks.

On a window in Iffley Church

December light shines through his torso,
the only flesh here exposed to human touch.
The rest is tastefully swathed in cloth
of elegant hue as befits a hero.
He remains opaque. His feet await
crucifixion or resurrection, not earth.
The hands, iconic, bless from their height
those who kneel at the two-candled altar.
His hair is lank and blond, well groomed.
His gentle eyes turn away to some other world.
If they were to make the window now,
he would be like a model,
selling, as it were, in a colour supplement,
some expensive perfume to cleanse
the stains of labouring humankind.

Light pours through the flesh onto the church.
It is the flesh, the flesh, forever given,
bestowing light and warmth, the touch of peace.

Under a swooning bird of grace,
the stranger stands in wonder.
Among the Romanesque arches,
he bows before the flesh on fire.
His flesh in need of love,
his flesh by flesh transfigured.

Meeting in Glenthorne

We met in silence, the cows and I
in the long wet grass, in worship they,
ruminating I. They sat. I stood
by the wooden fence that set apart
the sprawling house from the winding path
that climbed in awe to the passing clouds.
Again I saw the hill I climbed before:
angels ascending, descending,
stepping lightly on the unploughed earth.

From time to time the cows gave ministry
– a snort, a shuffling, a flick of tail.
I waited with cool reverence
upon the herd's hard wisdom.
Their eyes were heavy
with eternity and rain.
They sat with grace
upon the damp earth beneath.

Time enough for miracles.

Meetings

And so we sat down together.
We shared understandings, misunderstandings.
We hope for definitions, but did not find them.
We brought questions, long sculptured
in the studios of our days,
and tried to chisel meanings
in the workshops of our nights.

We wanted some response, oh some response.
Perhaps some came, somehow.
Some illumination, some passing cloud.
Some thunder came and departed
echoing our confusion. We shared
impossible thoughts, unbelievable words,
nightmares and daydreams.
We dared a touch of recognition.

Now we shall take leave of each other.
We shall bear on our shoulders,
sacks of reflections, suitcases of silence,
as heavy and as light as Christmas presents.

One day we shall unwrap them:
a kaleidoscope, a fountain,
a waterfall of glory,
all shades of the rainbow –
when the heart is ripe like an apple
and the season is golden and ready.

Oh give us the ripeness.
Oh bless us our seasons.

If asked what I was doing the day the news came out, I would say:

Finally before the end of the season
I lay in the damp November earth
as many bulbs as bodies waiting
for burial: chionodoxa, leucojam
(the giant variety), scilla,
and galanthus of three different kinds.

I watered them well. In Paris blood flowed.
I buried the bulbs in certain hope of spring,
a spring my sisters and my brothers will not see.
I covered them with earth as heavy
as prayer.

What have we done with our gods?

Anne Frank's House

When he came back from the camp, he asked
that the rooms remain bare, for lives
cannot be recreated, though the eye
searches for familiar patterns,
though the heart would remain heavy
at the final incompleteness
of it all. And she, the daughter,
learning to live behind drawn curtains,
would, no doubt, have wondered
why so many people from so many countries
would come to see how she and her family
almost lived here, fearful, not knowing.

In the cool of a November morning,
early to beat the crowds, we entered,
dutifully read the exhibition notices,
the reconstruction of diary excerpts,
the half-bidden, half-hidden comments
of one slowly learning what the world can offer:
emptiness and echoing stairs,
false partitions and curtains closed.
The bells of the Westerkerk still beat out the night,
like drums at a funeral procession along the canals.

And so, according to instructions, the rooms
are kept clear and the curtains kept drawn.
It is the visitor who brings the light and the darkness,

the hopes, seasons, moonlight and sunlight,
to this hidden place, this closed-up sanctuary,
where, in an untrammelled mind, a god
takes the shape of trees, blossoming with silence,
takes the form of continents still to discover.

Now we can draw the curtains. Light pours in.
We can open the doors. We can watch the leaves falling.
We can witness to years. We can greet
the bells tolling, tolling. We can hear,
without cowering, the prayer for the dead,
for those who returned, for the many who visit,
for those of us who bear in our hearts
the leaves, fallen, falling and yet to fall,
those hiding still behind the curtains of the mind,
drawn against the dawn, afraid of the sunlight.

So why did you go to Santiago?

to pray at the grave of a son of thunder
to find consolation in the nearness
to touch, to draw upon a passion
to harvest strength that grew from strength
to fill an emptiness

What did you find at Santiago?

there was a queue that never ended
there were a thousand silences
in a thousand tongues
a heavy cape with many jewels
a tomb silvered with aspiration

Why did you go to Santiago?

to offer thanks, to repair a fault,
to cure a wound, to curse a curse,
to remember a face, a caress of flesh
bereft of jewels
to reclaim a dream

What did you find at Santiago?

heavy stones and many tombs
mighty battles won and lost
altars and gods and enemies slain,
hands stretching out against the darkness
angels dancing in the street

Why did you go to Santiago?

because I had not been before
because the path was waiting for me
to see if I could walk in that direction
to see if my body could feel again
the pulse of yet another spring

What did you find at Santiago?

there were clothes hanging out to dry
boots broken by stone and mud
a column of fire burning before me
and columns of smoke that hid my back
heavy rain to cleanse the soul

Why did you go to Santiago?

to be close to, to be touched by
to be in another place that was not here
to join history, to escape geography
to review, to find again, to admire
to expect miracles

What did you find at Santiago?

a god perhaps? a people? a place to lay down
and to take up, to remove, and put on again,
a fire to burn soiled clothes and prayers
to hold before my smoke-filled eyes
a mirror to behold a stranger's face

Why did you go to Santiago?

because there was no other way
because it had always been there –
I went to reach the end of earth
where shells were waiting on the sand
for me to take upon my journey

What did you find at Santiago?

that the body has its needs
that the soul will not be forced
that little is required
that the living need their rest
as do the dead

that the dead also need to move
as we the living do.

Narcissus

He knelt over the pool. Hushed
the wood and the world. The pounding only.
The machine in the breast. He
waited. Eyes closed. There was,
it seemed, a moon somewhere above.
This time, made timid by memory,
this time slowly, he opened his eyes
to behold not a flower but a sea
of tears. Never having learned to swim,
he fell deep. To drown in his own reflection.

2020 Poems of Confinement

Still

This earth is the same earth, is it not,
which we traversed with determination,
where, in former times, we ventured forth,
when travel was permitted, and choice was ours
over time and destination? This earth
now proclaims a different dominion.
It cries out now from the fissures
we have torn in it, from the scars
we have clawed in it, from the brutality
of our embrace, our craving for conquest.

Yet we, defeated by victory, remain apart
until in the bowels of the earth we bury our dead,
and scatter our ashes in its still fertile loam.
Still even now it is ready to receive us.

We are its children, are we not, made of its flesh,
dust of its dust? Our hearts beat to its rhythms.
We spin as the earth spins. Though we tasted the fruit
of the tree of knowledge, and Eden became exile,
we remain the offspring of its seasons.
Still the earth offers us ground for our planting,
generous still if we would grow wise and tender,
earth for our planting, trees for our healing,
a new, a fragile, an abundant harvest. Still.

Time between Times

This is the time between times. A time when
yesterday has fallen to nostalgia, and tomorrow
fails imagination. Familiar places where we walked,
talked, sat, rested our bodies and minds
have become places of impossible pilgrimage.
They rise up through sleep in the middle of the night
before we recall this confining space, this enclosing moment.
Faces appear out of the early hours, words form
that we should have said, did not say, should not have said.
We fashion ghosts out of foreboding.

There were temples where we met to worship,
and fruit trees forbidden that we dared to touch
and we sailed around the world in arks and drowned
in the exodus sea and saw, if only for a brief moment,
a promised land inhabited already by the myriads of our
longings.

But. Today I hear the birds. I am reminded that flight is
possible,
and song can be heard across fields, across rivers. I recall
the sound of voices, the accents of my days, the languages
I have crossed. They crowd me, they create me.
Now they are the beakers from which I drink what of light
is still possible, the dawn, the heat of midday, the close
of noon, the failing sun, the silent cry of night.
This is a time between times, the only time
in which I can live, and move, and have my being.

It is always between.

A day of Visitation

Each day is a day of visitation, an encounter, a moment of
choice.
Each blade of grass pierces the flesh, and ray of sun,
blinding,
burns deep into the mind's eye. Angels descend.
They announce the child within. It is a day of judgement.
The body within this tomb may rise or fall
for good or ill. And I may turn my hand this way
or that, open or closed, to hold
or tear apart – my heart, open or closed, to receive
or turn aside the message they offer. The choice is mine.

                    The bloom of the cherry tree,
open for a sacred while, grows from month to month, from
death
to life to underfoot. You have visited me with the full white
of flower,
have sung to me in the blackbird, have called my name
in each passing cloud. You have met me in the cold wind and
in the moonlight,
and in the multitudes of winged stars. You name me time
and time again.
You lay a table spread out before me. I wait and I wonder.
I walk and I lie down. I hear the river and the ocean.
They call. The flower and the thorn. "The choice is yours",
you proclaim.

And from somewhere deep within my bones,
a child is summoned, brought forth, turning this way and
that,
overwhelmed by the grass and the light and the judgement of
angels.

The child takes me by the hand, looks deep into my eyes.
"What are you doing at this time, in this place?
How are you walking upon the earth?
What healing? What healing?"

Rye Pilgrimage 2020

On his return from the Camino de Compostela
he fastened a shell to his backpack
to remind him that each step was pilgrimage.

There were stars to follow and signs by the roadside,
many a guide with anecdotes and legends,
footsteps carved deep into the earth.

Throughout his life there were journeys undertaken
to shrines, ruins, where hermits and madmen
had found the consolation or hardship they craved for.

There was Jerusalem and he wept on Zion Mount
and at Yad Vashem where a candle was reflected
in many tiny flames.

There was Holy Island where the sheep bore witness
and at dawn a heron joined him for worship
at the rising of the sun.

There was Walsingham. He knelt in the holy house,
built according to the instructions
of an improbable dream.

There were banners high
on his march through London.
They demanded peace, an end to lamentation.

There was the house of Anne Frank
where betrayal brought death. After her words,
only silence was possible.

There was the camp in Gaza
Where he spoke of his origins, could offer only
his lamentations.

There was Iona, and the western saints,
a fortress against the tide. He longed again
for illumination.

The old meeting houses of South Jersey,
where the Friends had gathered
to realise the kingdom.

Now the roads are blocked
and the sky is limited
and footsteps counted.

He leaves the house and walks
the short path to where
honesty flowers among the maples.

Beyond the yucca and the rosebush,
the armoury and the tollhouse,
the path grows sacred.

Again the path leads inwards,
past the bluebells and the cow parsley.
He honours the nettles.

Dandelions and butterbur,
periwinkles and violets,
stations of the cross.

The rising and the falling,
the rebirth of beech and horse chestnut,
forget me not.

A journey beyond bramble,
horsetail, to where
lords and ladies hold court.

Among the nettles and the celandine,
an intimate pilgrimage.
None the less holy.

No given name. No guide.
No sacred text.
Just signs of grace along the roadside.

Passover*

This meal is our escape from slavery.
We eat of the bitter herbs and dare to sing,
we, the people who made bricks with straw,
who saw the overseers draw blood
from the backs of our children and had to keep silent.
With torn nails we built temples for Pharaoh.
They are in ruin now. We live on. We sing.

A dark angel stalked the city.
We smeared blood on the posts of our doors
as a sign for the curse to pass over.
Their children and their rivers ran red with blood.
We fled far into the bowels of the desert
and they and their horses drowned behind us.
We are told to rejoice.

And yet, we turn and remember.
We lust for what we lost,
the comforts, certainties, the knowledge.
We mourn the friends we left behind
among the people who broke us. We grieve
for the horses who were drowned, for the people
who hid us in the day of persecution.

I dip my finger into the glass of wine,
pour out ten drops in memory
of the ten plagues that befell them.
I find my own blood on the plate.

At the table now there is an empty chair
for our awaited guest, the restless prophet.
His face is the face of those we have not invited
to sit at this table, the face of many nations.

"No", he announces, "you are not a people apart.
You are not immune from the plagues of Egypt.
You have raised Pharaohs amongst you,
built prisons, enslaved your children in tales
that tell only of enemies and persecution.
You went out frightened into deserts
but did not find the thorn that burns.
No mountain of revelation trembled before you.
With the treasures you rescued, you built
gods of silver and gold copied from your masters
and worshipped them in imitation.
You carried your Egypt branded upon you.
How then shall you sing?"

Air has turned to breathlessness,
fields are covered with barrenness,
slavery has returned and the earth cries
under the burden of our lives. We are still in exile,
exiled from our dreams, exiled from our daily lives.

Yet, tonight in this meal of remembrance,
this night, which is different from all other nights,
this night at this time of pestilence,
we dare, with the song of songs, to sing of spring.

Today we listened to the distant birds
and watched them fly beyond the clouds.
Tonight, we look up to behold as in a desert sky
the bright companionship of many stars.
By their light we behold the remembered faces
of friends, of strangers who offered consolation
on the journey whose destination we never discovered.
By their distant radiance we gaze again
on the face of the earth that gave us life
and dare as its children to dream old dreams
and to chant old tales of breaking free.

Next year in a new city, by a new river,
we shall take down our harps and play new music,
and drink a wine that tastes of sunlight.
We shall gather the wild herbs that grow in profusion
the bitter and the sweet. We shall break
a bread that is no longer of affliction
and share its bounty with a world in waiting.

This earth is the bread of rejoicing.
Each tree is aflame. Each soul I meet
though now at a distance, is the prophet
I am waiting for. Each morning
over a world still shrouded in darkness
the doves sing in the tentative sunlight.

**"My beloved spoke and said to me,
  "Arise, my darling,
  my beautiful one, come with me.
See! The winter is past;
  the rains are over and gone.
Flowers appear on the earth;
  the season of singing has come,
the cooing of doves
  is heard in our land.
The fig tree forms its early fruit;
  the blossoming vines spread their fragrance.
Arise, come, my darling;
  my beautiful one, come with me."

* Passover was originally a spring festival marking the return of fertility after the winter. The Passover meal, as celebrated in Jewish households today, involves through word and song the retelling and reliving of the exodus of the Israelites from Egypt. The story goes from slavery to liberation which become the archetype of all stories of hope. During the meal, matzoh, unleavened bread is eaten, as are bitter herbs and wine is drunk. During the proceedings ten drops of wine are spilled in memory of the ten plagues that befell the oppressors. A chair is left empty for the prophet Elijah, the precursor of redemption.

** Song of Songs 2, 10-13.

Instructions for survival – Voice in my Head

1.

When you go out, carry I.D.

– you have to prove who you are.

When you drive,

make sure they see

your licence, your papers

– you have to prove this life is yours.

Don't play music too loud,

that's for white kids,

not for you.

Get out of the way

when asked to do so,

especially by men in uniform

– that proves you know your place,

which is not here.

Don't answer back.

Look to the ground.

Don't be too flash.

Don't show emotions,

Don't feel too strongly.

When you protest,

remember we are always polite

in this country.

Don't go out at night.

Don't cover your head.

Don't wear a mask,
unless there is a plague,
– you have to prove somehow
you are socially acceptable.

2.
When you go out, bury your heart
so they can't see it
on your sleeve. Don't
touch your friend too close
or laugh too loud
or walk in ways which show.
Control the butterflies
of your hands.
Don't stare too hard.
Don't speak of him or her
which might reveal
an unnatural interest
an abnormal desire.

At all times remain
appropriate, your comments
apposite, your interests
adequate. Don't shock
the priest. The rabbi won't like it.
The imam won't invite you back.
Don't confuse the guru
or make the pastor tremble.
Don't embarrass the teacher
or the horses.

Don't talk too much of love,
No, not that, they know
what that is, not you.
You only feel it
in the marrow of your bones,
in the ache of your stomach.

My sister, my brother,
you want to survive, don't you?
But how do you learn which uniform
will not imprison you,
which passer-by is your ally?
How will you know
which priest will bless you,
which rabbi will marry you,
which imam will bestow gifts
upon your loving?

3.
Ah, but if you want really to live,
you will have to go down to the streets
and make your backpack of mistakes.
Carry a medicine chest with you
for the wounds you will receive.

Surviving is not living.
The choice, this time,
Is yours.
Dream

We are living a dream, but not living the dream
they taught us to live, in a dream house,
with a paradise garden, and statistical children.

Sure, this world where now we venture
partakes of, has the texture of dream.
It mirrors the world where we lived. The streets are the same.
The houses have retained their shape. The same birds sing.

But if we walk at all, our steps echo the silence.
We walk like ghosts, swathed, distant, locked in this
other sort of dream, where time has lost its shape

and days have lost their sequence
and hands cannot reach out
and many starve for touch and food or sky.

Somewhere we feel there is a timetable,
an agenda, an order of service, a way of doing things
we cannot quite remember. Something eludes.

It is like the life we lived, but with a different smell.
There is a muffled flatness of things
as when we lie in bed at three in the morning

and our fingers are numb and our back aches
and there are no signs in the sky. It is an interlude in living,
and silence weighs heavy upon our chest.

Haunted by years and places we can no longer visit,
the people we were, and may not see again,
we watch the clock and count the hours.

At this unearthly hour, on this unearthly day,
as was our custom before the dream began,
we look for hope in the eastern sky.

A feeble sun announces dawn. Intimations
of times before, when we could plan our lives.
We lie, we wake, we sleep. We dream awhile.

Day will rise.

Autumn Trees and Crows, a painting by Wang Hui

The little house by the steam looks more beautiful at dusk.
The autumn trees around the eve gather shadowy crows.
I wonder when we can meet again,
so together we can drink tea by the cold light.

Tang Yin (1470-1524)

a cottage, scarcely visible, framed by twisted branches
a man, minuscule, crosses the water,
crows, tiny, middle plane
an unfolding sky
in the cold night we said our farewells
you bowed from the bridge as you left
in the direction of the hall in which I lingered
shutters open in spite of the wind

you will be forever on the bridge
as crows will forever fly
the shutters drawn apart
my eyes on the water between us, forever

Bamboo

Zheng Xie claimed it took him forty years
to get this far in the painting of bamboos,
the way the leaves hung, the darkness,
the light, the stems, the rock behind.

'Bamboo in my eyes. Bamboo in my heart.
Bamboo in my hands.' The green of things,
the way the poem framed the scroll,
the way the rock aspired.

To see, to feel, to create.
The hand moved across the page,
invisible. The sweat across his brow.
Passion in the unmoving wind.

To spend one's life on the one task,
turning one's back on the facile technique,
embracing the vision of how to hold the brush,
how to hold the leaf before it dies.

Pedragalejo. Prayer

Each day, before this time began,
before the beach was cordoned off
and policemen guarded sand and sea,
he came alone to shore and sun,
and crawled across the broken rocks
to find a place to hold him firm.
He sat where sea, and sky, and cloud alone
might fill his eyes, his arms outstretched.

One day a cormorant came into view;
the next, out, out to sea a sail;
the next, a sudden revelation
of overwhelming sunlight. Words
were washed away like footmarks on sand.
He closed his eyes. An unvoiced cry
from deep within, a letting go, a giving up.
"All that I ever was, to all that ever is".

The light was tendered.
The sun turned rose.
The night fell softly,
from dark to light
and light to dark

the silence
and the lapping waves.

Song Thrush

Except for one or two of the commonest birds I really cannot distinguish between bird song. The other morning however I found a website of the songs of the ten most common birds. I was particularly enchanted by the song of the song thrush. It seems to follow a pattern of a melody which it repeats three or four times before going onto a different one. This morning I was listening to Radio 3 where someone had uploaded a song of a thrush heard early this morning near Bristol. It was truly riveting and it brought me close to tears.

As I sat this morning in a Quaker meeting where each of us were separate in our own homes this morning because of the lockdown I thought of the song as a sort of prayer: at first a song of gratitude; second time a song which seemed to suggest *I'm not sure if you're there please listen to my prayer,* a third time: *I'm doing this again because I really want you to hear;* a fourth time: *I'm not sure whether anyone is listening but I'm still going to sing with the whole of my being because I am a song thrush.* And I thought what a wonderful theologian the little thrush is.

Grief

Joe Jones, the editor of the Friend magazine, ended an article with the words: "Our first responsibility, then, is to grieve."

Yes, I grieve, not out of duty, or because I feel I ought, but because I am part of the cycle of things, their pain, their birth, their death.

Yes, I grieve each evening at 6 pm when the news begins again, when tired faces speak the facts they cannot understand, when the numbers fall upon me like lava from an inevitable volcano.

Yes, I grieve, and touch my partner's hand, and think, so far, yes, we have reached so far. We, for the time being, are here.

Yes, I grieve, for the numbers I cannot comprehend, and the faces I have never known, the names I do not recognise, and the ones who love them, loved them and called their names.

Yes, I grieve, for those who visit my mind from the rooms of almost oblivion, who have touched my life, and I wonder…

Yes, I grieve already that when we leave this house of confinement, we may meet again the old greed, bitterness, the fears that we have known so often in the old world.

Yes, I grieve, at the old walls, fences, frontiers, grieve that our hopes may be snatched from us, dashed to earth.

Yes, I grieve, but at this time I also know that grief is a sign of love, and that love can give birth to hope, and that without hope we cannot live.

I grieve, therefore I love.
I love, therefore I hope.
I can do no other.

I lift up my eyes

I lift up my eyes to the hills
where like a god, the sun
shows its face and hides its meaning.
I watch its slow birth in the morning,
watch it grow. It fades away
with my dreams in the evening sky.

The one who watches over you
will not slumber; will not
let you slumber or sleep,
will be your companion,
is the shade at your right hand,
is the shadow upon your soul.

I have lifted my eyes and have seen
prophets and angels
ascending and descending,
bearing gifts, many fine words
and many instructions.
Their wisdom is a rock bruising my heart.

Why do the leaders rage,
and princes rise up against their people?
They order their subjects to temples,
to pray quietly to their silent gods,
muzzle with steel their mouths,
their mourning, their lamentation.

We lift up our eyes, we dare to scan
the peaks of the mountains,
the eastern sky of promise,
the western sky of anger.
We do not need tablets of stone
with yet more incantations.

In our rebellion and our grief,
we rise, we soar like eagles.
We lift up our eyes to the hills
where help has been promised.
A ragged man descends.
He has broken the tablets.

This land, this earth

This great land is mine,
he cried, shaking history like a spear.
These mountains belong to my tribe.
These figs, these vines, hills,
are my inheritance.

We sat and watched.
We broke our silence:
We belong to the earth our mother.
We do not own. We are owned
By the vast sky and its clouds.

Birds were flying high over the broken walls.

What remains

A lifetime ago. What remains:
a summer camp, a poem recited,
(Leopardi on the passing of things).
Warm days, collecting rags for charity
(recycling was not a word we knew yet).
Songs in the evening from the Italian resistance.
Turin. 1967 or 1968?
Furio from Pula.
The music of your name plays in my memory.
Pula, the site of a great Roman cemetery.
Furio, your name like breath
hovers over the gravestones.

Harry

A brief meeting over a pint.
You had fled the tanks in Budapest.
You settled here. Somewhere, I forget,
or didn't you tell me?
Off ship for an hour or two.
Something of your life flickered across
as you touched my fingers.
I did come back the other evening.
Your ship must have sailed away.
Both at sea.

Visitations from childhood

A candlestick half-lit on a makeshift altar.
The world and its winds whispered urgently
through the window he could not close.

Piled high on the table, his books remained half-read,
books his heart, his mind had sanctified. He waited.

He watched the flames, the sky. Scraps of prayer
formed, unravelled. He covered his head,
consorting as he was with his god and with angels.

His face shone with awe. Beyond the flaking walls,
the world and its chatter spun round to tempt him.

He muttered the verses. He waited. He watched.
Messiahs walked through the flames. Angels
fanned his brow with giant wings. Enchanting.

In this room, flames beckoned him to his altar.
Outside, in faltering light, the winds called him by name.

The world and its flames will enter his sanctuary.
Angels will lure him into the shining streets of the town.
He will follow them, half-obedient to the beating of their
wings.

Today

What have I done today?
What have I not done?

I went to the temple.
I tried to learn wisdom.

I went to the meadow
to empty my mind.

I read all the books I could find.
I pillaged their stories.

I watched some great programmes.
I came away blinded with tears.

I went to the meetings.
I heard the most profound of speakers.

As I walked home alone,
the questions grew louder.

What have I not done today?
What have I done?

Today like yesterday
children lie hungry.

Tomorrow like today,
old women will sleep in the gutter.

Today like every day,
plagues will reap their harvest.

The planet will still spin,
forests will burn more brightly.

Today like every day,
I shall try to find words for prayer.

The same god will hear
or choose to remain silent.

What did I see today?
Where did I go today?

Whom did I meet today?
What did I say

that made any difference at all
to the pain, to the tears of things?

I can only lift up my eyes
and lift up my fists to the clouds.

My aching legs will carry me a little.
My tired eyes will scan horizons.

I must be the book I read,
the poem I write, the silence.

I am the meeting to attend,
the work to accomplish,

for I am the hungry child,
the refugee and her boat.

We drown together
or land on unwelcoming soil.

I must learn to utter what is given
to this mouth, these hands.

To write down the words
the angel is dictating.

I must discover the reason
I have been given breath today.

Breath   *almost a prayer*

tentative   early morning light
eyes opening slowly   this room   this time
your breathing   a recognised rhythm

gratitude   gradually   for the here
and the now   the body unfurls   like a leaf

thoughts in battalions   wait
impatiently   the slightest entrance   the waking mind

he remembers a god   he digs deep in the well
of his heart   to find the words   any words

breath is all   the dance of things
a melody recalled   from another time   another place

the only words I can offer thee:
I cannot hold thee with words
just my breathing   our breathing   ever

A sort of epiphany

We did not think we were wise, though we had,
it is true, a certain power and status in our lands.
We met in our palaces, over wine and music,
to discern the best ways to govern
both the world and our passions.
We never really found any answers
to the questions we asked of each other.

                                    One night as usual
we were scouring the heavens looking for signs.
We beheld an unknown star and perplexed fell silent.
We consulted, of course, but none could explain it.
Then one of us, I cannot remember which,
suggested something unexpected. We were not
to ask the learned nor read in their books.
We would try an experiment (a task normally
entrusted to servants). We would take a journey.
We would follow the light. We would risk everything
(though we would need a caravan and guards to protect us).
We would take gifts for the people who guarded the star.

We visited a palace of course. We understood royalty.
There we found a fearful king and the star pointed in an-
other direction.
We were led to an inn in a poor part of town.
The mud dirtied our boots and tunics.
We were led to a baby, not the vision expected.

There was a cry, a young mother, straw on the dirty floor.
There were animals and low people smelling of flocks.
Was this filth the outcome of our confabulations?
Was this child the magus for the gold and the myrrh
– frankincense to overcome the smells of a stable?
Was this the revelation promised in our dreams,
new life among smells, a flashing star, peasants
speaking an incomprehensible language?

We returned home without a map and a band of restive
servants.
In our palaces fearfully, we renewed our conversations.
We decided to ignore omens written in the sky.
We would to stay in our halls and close the doors behind us.
Something stirred within us however. The wine of our meetings
had a different taste, the music a different savour.
When we met in the evenings, we felt like accomplices.
We listened to each other's voices with greater attention.
We embraced the silence we offered each other.

We put aside our robes of satin. We put away the gold of our
crowns.
We were tired. We were afraid of new journeys.
For the rest of our lives, we have sat and have waited.
We remember the straw and the mud,
the words in languages we could not understand.
There is always a child crying, a star flickering in the night sky.

Zooming for worship

We come with heart and mind and device prepared.
We click. We wait. We test the sound. Await our fate.
We gain admittance. Familiar faces, familiar places. We
smile.
Some sigh. Some close their eyes. Some mute.
Alone together in a world where we cannot touch,
we touch with heart and soul. Though mute we greet.
Though "Internet connection is unstable", we are able to
connect.
Words and silences cross the space between. Some
consolation,
some anticipation of a life resumed, some reminiscence
of how it used to be before and might well be again.

Exchanging news, we are reminded of the day
when we could shake each other's hand, announce
that coffee will be made, invite each Friend for this and that.
We shall meet next week if we are spared, they used to say.

He said there was an ocean of night
but even greater was the light,
– more magnificent still
the deeper sight of what will be again.

Juvenalia revised in age

Mirror

The mirror showed the lines
the years had scratched across.

Her fingers in the hold of a cigarette
numbered the deeds of her hands:

the book written, the manifestoes signed,
hours and hours of public speaking.

Her lips that blew our smoke,
pinching and pursing,

recalled meetings addressed,
many reasons for changing the world.

On her table, first lines of a poem:
"I would give up all worlds

to be young and in love
and walking again by the river."

She could not end the poem.
The metre escaped her.

To his muse

She has left me
after several years
we lived together,
more or less, ate
at the same table.

We met when I
was too young
and though my game
was that of an amateur
(and perhaps has remained so)
I loved her deeply.
Not that I alone enjoyed her nights
or she alone my days
but in her fashion
and I in mine, we loved
and almost deeply.

Sometimes she returns
for a limited conversation,
perhaps to reminisce,
and holds my mind
and holds my hand
and leads me on,
a little, as before,
But I grow bored
by her airs and graces.

I forget the next steps
of our mutual game
and fall asleep
by the evening fire.

Bisperode.

1

Night falls uncertain on long green fields.
Somewhere there is an enchanted castle,
woven in a tapestry of thee and me.
Warp and weft embrace in sleep.

2

And so we lie who scarcely dared
to touch and to be in peace.
There may be wars within our hearts
as were once waged across these fields.
We shall be disarmed
whose arms were crossed in love.

3

This was not meant to be
this falling into arms
this drowning in eyes
this making of memories.
It was not timetabled
between planes and trains and expectations.
There was a touch, oh yes,
a hope, a smile, words half understood.

This is the risk we take
when once we love.

Haiku of light and experience

Rich, orange the sun.
The old man, supple as grass,
turns in sacred flame.

*

After clouds of words,
he walks out in the night.
Sea and sand shine blue.

*

Keen we watch at noon.
Deserts of grey block out the sky.
Lit by stars within.

*

Your light dazzles me,
leaves me blind as blackened glass.
Let me reflect you.

*

We sit by pale trees.
Doves fly by with light for wings,
announcing spirit.

*

Cowslips play with sun.
Hyacinths shine blue with sky.
All bodies hold light.

*

You come bringing peace.
Caps of mist hide mountain tops.
Light pools in your tracks.
                *

We talk hours of light.
Words congregate like locusts.
Day unbidden dawns.

His eyes are flame. His
fingers point the way, which
glows beneath our feet.
                *

Winter jasmine waits.
Wind and snow and pale sunlight
proclaim its rebirth.
                *

Like an old man's tear,
a winter sun hangs on the sea.
We hoist shipwrecked dreams.
                *

Alleys spin back years.
Long gowns rustle in sunlight.
Exile was his home.

She remembers songs.
A ship took her to new lands.
Their flutes were her pain.
                *

Mimosa trembles.
On a cool evening she waits.
Light peals like a bell.
*

This calm slope in frost.
Its whole vast diversity.
The blue and green planet.
*

You touch my shoulder.
A brief ministry, a smile.
Behold, it's dawn.
*

Bamboo yields to breeze.
A bird call, insistent, shrill.
It is the first day.
*

For next year's birth,
plant when flower fails, leaf falls.
Yield them to their moon.
*

Silence shades the hill.
Clouds hide the sun. Her hands plant
exotic orchids.
*

Among the hot rubble
children play their parents' games.
I shoot and you fall.
                    *

The wind blows fierce here.
Variegated holly bends.
Tossed branches form prayers.
                    *

Long years of training.
Long nights of wild speculation.
Burning straw at dawn.
                    *

You sit by the sea.
You pipe your song to the wind.
Waves roar their reply.
                    *

They plant red tulips
in plastic pots, neat in threes.
Their very leaves scream.

God came down today,
poured through the stained glass windows,
stained stone with blood.
                    *

Suddenly I saw.
Your calm eyes were white with sky.
My soul leapt within.
*

The lord's my shepherd.
I, the goat, the mountain lion.
Leave your staff and jump.
*

Weary travellers
put destination on hold.
And the geese fly south.

We come from far. We
lay before you our incense.
We return; not wise.

Wind chases the clouds.
Human strivings quail and quake.
Gales blow where they will.

On the horizon,
dark trees shake like old men.
Is there time enough?

We build strong fences
to keep the wild soul bulls out.
Lions scorn our hands.

An early stranger
examines the snow mountains.
They are where they were.

The great hall awaits.
Words pile on words to the beams.
Coffin or ladder?

We are the children
of desert pilgrimages.
Light begins to fall.

We have waited long
by the gate called beautiful.
Light pours from the cracks.

On the altar now
the offering lies waiting.
Clouds pass over. Mute.

The lilac season.
Days grow heavy in the soil.
Desire like seedlings.

Missing a thermal,
the seagull flaps in panic.
Let go. Let your wings.

Blackthorn marks the path.
Clouds scurry across the hills.
We shed fears like rain.

You ask for wonders.
How many rainbows must I
bring to your locked cell?

I have seen your face
before in covered mirrors.
Masks. Skeleton keys.

"That tree is not wild enough".
Magnolia stellata.
But I was vanquished.

Priest behind a mask.
Hands rubbed clean for blessing. Still
the wild dove descends.

You ask for my faith.
I offer you this haiku.
Mind, heart, soul. Loving.

Lightning Source UK Ltd.
Milton Keynes UK
UKHW022059270221
379494UK00009B/190